Space Scientist
THE MOON

Heather Couper and Nigel Henbest

Franklin Watts
London New York Toronto Sydney

© 1986 Franklin Watts

First published in 1986 by
Franklin Watts
12a Golden Square
London W1R 4BA

First published in the USA
by Franklin Watts Inc.
387 Park Avenue South
New York, N.Y. 10016

First published in Australia
by Franklin Watts
Australia
14 Mars Road
Lane Cove, NSW 2066

UK ISBN: 0 86313 472 6
US ISBN: 0-531-10266-1
Library of Congress
Catalog Card No:
86-50350

Illustrations by
Drawing Attention
Rhoda Burns
Rob Burns
Eagle Artists
Michael Roffe

Photographs by
NASA

Designed by
David Jefferis

Printed in Belgium

Space Scientist

THE MOON

Contents

Earth and Moon

Look up at the sky at night, and the chances are that you will see the brilliant face of the Moon looking back down. The Moon is the second brightest object in our skies, after the Sun, and at night the Moon completely outshines all the stars and planets. At its brightest, when it is Full, the Moon throws shadows and provides enough light for us to read by.

In ancient times, travelers regarded the Moon as a friend, because it lit up the dark nights and reduced the risk of an attack by highwaymen.

The Moon appears so big and bright in the sky simply because it is so close to the Earth. At a distance of 384,400 km (238,900 miles), the Moon is less than one-hundredth the distance of the next closest object, the planet Venus. Despite its brightness, the Moon has no light of its own. It shines just because it is reflecting the Sun's light.

Unlike the planets, the Moon does not go around the Sun. It follows an orbit around the Earth, like the artificial satellites that have been launched by rockets into Earth-orbit. For this reason, the Moon is sometimes called Earth's natural satellite.

Some planets have many natural satellites. If we lived on Jupiter, for example, we would see 16 moons in the sky. Astronomers have searched for other moons going around the Earth, but they have not found any, and it seems that our planet has just the one Moon.

The Moon is a much smaller world than the Earth. With a diameter of 3,476 km (2,160 miles), the Moon is only a quarter as large as our planet. It would take 81 Moons to weigh as much as the Earth. Because the Moon contains so little matter, its gravity is much weaker than that of the Earth. If you stood on the Moon, you would weigh only one-sixth of what you weigh on the Earth: on the Moon, a high-jumper would be able to jump over a house!

The Earth has an atmosphere because its gravity holds on to gases like oxygen and

▷ A "moonscape" (far right) is totally unlike a view on Earth. Our familiar blue sky is due to sunlight being scattered by the air. The Moon has no air, so the Sun beats down from a jet-black sky. Without air, there is no water, and no plants or animals. Astronauts, carrying their own air supplies, move about by "kangaroo-hopping" in the Moon's weak gravity.

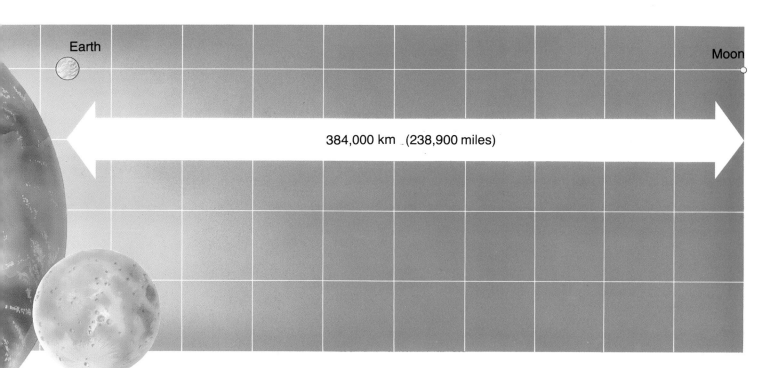

Earth

Moon

384,000 km (238,900 miles)

◁ The Moon is quite small when compared to the Earth (about one-quarter its size), but it is large as compared, for example, to the planet Pluto.

△ The Moon goes around the Earth at an average distance of 384,400 km (238,900 miles). Its actual distance varies from 364,400 km (226,400 miles) at its closest to 406,700 km (252,700 miles). A beam of light, or a radio wave, takes nearly three seconds to travel to the Moon and back.

nitrogen and prevents them from escaping into the vacuum of space. The Moon's gravity is too weak to hold on to any bases, so the Moon is completely airless. When astronauts land on the Moon's barren surface, they must take their own air to breathe.

Because there is no air, there can be no water on the Moon either: liquid water would immediately boil away into the vacuum. There are no rivers, lakes or seas. The lack of air and water means that no living things – plants or animals – have managed to evolve on the Moon.

Without a blanket of air, the Moon's surface is exposed to the harsh conditions of space. Its unprotected surface is covered in crater scars from meteorite impacts. Some impacts were so severe that lava from deep inside the Moon welled up to fill the holes. The Moon's rocks freeze, to a temperature of −155°C (−310°F), when it is night-time on the Moon and the surface is exposed to the cold of space. But during the lunar day, the Sun's heat beats on the unprotected rocks, and bakes them to 105°C (220°F) – above the boiling point of water.

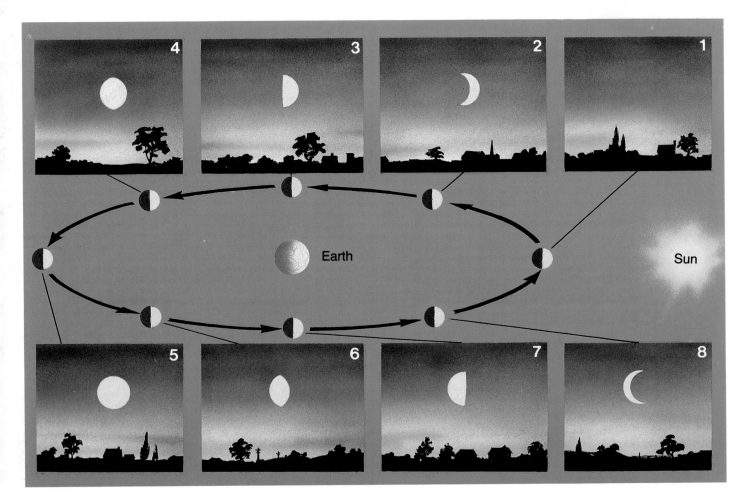

Phases of the Moon

When we look at the Moon in the sky, its shape seems to change from night to night. These changes – the Moon's phases – have nothing to do with the Moon itself. They are due to the way in which our view of the sunlit part of the Moon alters as the Moon goes around the Earth.

The Moon has no light of its own. The Sun lights it up, illuminating just the half that is facing toward the Sun. When we look at the Moon, we can see only the sunlit part of it.

At the time of New Moon, the Moon lies in the same direction as the Sun. We are looking toward the unlit side of the Moon, and as a result we cannot see it at all. A few days later, the Moon has moved around in its orbit, and we can just see a narrow region of the lit-up side, forming a crescent in the evening sky.

The amount of the Moon visible then increases, or waxes. A week after New Moon,

the Moon has gone a quarter of the way around its orbit, and it is the time of first Quarter, when we see half the Moon lit up. After this, we see more than half the Moon illuminated, and it is called gibbous.

Two weeks after New Moon, the Moon is Full. All of the illuminated face is turned toward us, and the Moon appears as a complete glowing disc. After Full Moon, we see less and less of the illuminated side, and the Moon appears to shrink, or wane, past Last Quarter and crescent, back to the next New Moon.

The Moon rises and sets just like the Sun as the Earth rotates. The time of moonrise and moonset depends on the phase. This means that we see the waxing Moon in the evening sky and the waning Moon in the morning sky. Although the Moon is most prominent at night, it is often above the horizon during the day.

△ A Polar Orbiter separates from a relay satellite, high over the Moon in the 1990s. Below the spacecraft is the heavily cratered far side of the Moon, which is never visible from the Earth's surface. The Polar Orbiter will take pictures of the far side, and of the Moon's poles.

Sometimes when the Moon is a thin crescent, we can see the dark regions glowing faintly, as "the old Moon in the new Moon's arms." This is due to the Sun's light being reflected off the Earth, on to the dark side of the Moon.

The Moon takes 27.3 days to go around the Earth, if we time the period it takes to come back to the same position as seen against the distant stars. But the time from one Full Moon to the next is rather longer – 29.5 days. This is because the Full Moon occurs when the Sun and Moon are in opposite directions as seen from the Earth. By the time the Moon has returned to exactly the same position relative to the stars, the Earth has moved around its curved orbit about the Sun, and the Sun is no longer opposite to the Moon's position. The Moon must move a bit further around its orbit to reach a position opposite to the Sun.

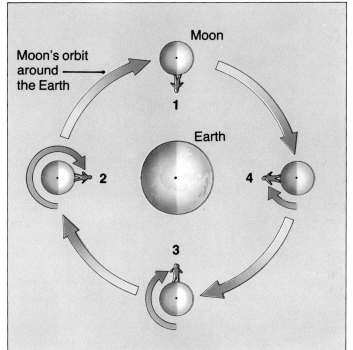

△ The same side of the Moon *always* faces the Earth. If an astronaut stood still in the middle of this side (1), then the Moon's rotation would swing him round by 90° as the Moon moves 90° around its orbit (2), so he would still appear to be directly facing us. This continues round the orbit (3 and 4).

Tides

Everyone who has been to the seaside or a seaport knows that the level of the sea rises and falls twice a day, obliterating sandcastles when it rises to high tide, and leaving boats high and dry as it falls to low tide. What is not so obvious is that the Moon is responsible for the movement of the tides.

The Moon is a much smaller body than the Earth, and so it has a much weaker gravity. But even so, the Moon's gravity has an effect on the Earth. The Moon pulls on the Earth to such an extent that it is not quite correct to say that the Moon goes around the center of the Earth: in fact, both the Earth and the Moon go around a balance point.

Because the Earth has the more powerful gravity, the balance point is much closer to the center of the Earth than to the center of the Moon. This balance point actually lies just inside the surface of the Earth.

Because the Earth is swinging around this balance point, there is a centrifugal force that tries to throw everything in a direction away from the Moon. This is balanced by the pull of the Moon's gravity.

If the Moon's gravity were the same at all distances from the Moon, then there would be no overall effect – and no tides. The Moon's gravity would everywhere balance the centrifugal force exactly, and the two forces would cancel out.

But the strength of the Moon's gravity (like that of any object) falls off the farther we get from the Moon. On the side of the Earth furthest away from the Moon, the Moon's gravity is weaker than the centifugal force, and the centrifugal force pulls the Earth's surface outward. On the side of the Earth facing the Moon, on the other hand, the Moon's gravity is stronger than the centrifugal force, and it pulls the Earth's surface upward and outward. As a result, the Earth's surface bulges outward in two directions: directly away from the Moon, and directly toward the Moon.

We don't notice the bulges in the Earth's surface, in fact, because the rocks making up the Earth are quite rigid, and do not deform much. On the other hand, the water in the oceans feels the same forces, and it can move freely to form much bigger bulges.

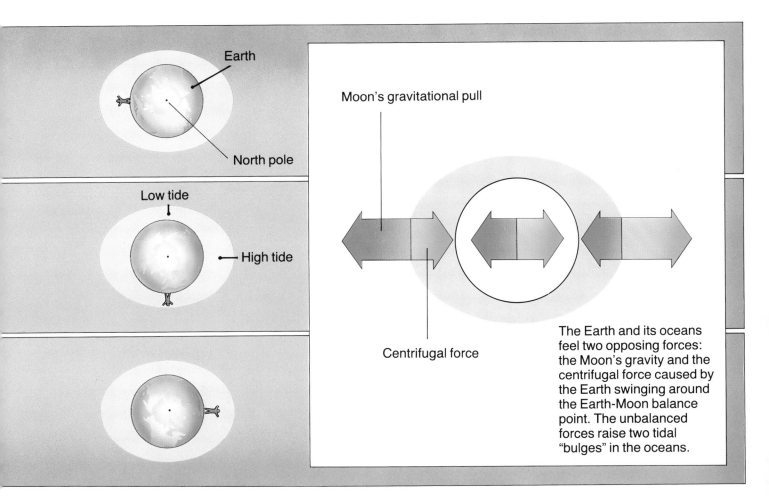

Earth

North pole

Low tide

High tide

Moon's gravitational pull

Centrifugal force

The Earth and its oceans feel two opposing forces: the Moon's gravity and the centrifugal force caused by the Earth swinging around the Earth-Moon balance point. The unbalanced forces raise two tidal "bulges" in the oceans.

△ Each seaport or seaside resort experiences two high tides a day: as the Earth spins round, it carries every point on its surface under the two "tidal bulges" in the oceans, one facing the Moon, the other pointing directly away. The tidal bulges move gradually around the Earth, following the Moon in its orbit.

As the Earth rotates, once a day, your particular part of the coast moves under first one bulge, and then the other, to produce the two high tides of the day.

The two tidal bulges, on either side of the Earth, act like giant brake shoes. Friction between the water and the ocean floor slows down the rate at which the Earth is turning, and so increases the length of the Earth's day – at a rate of a thousandth of a second every century. To compensate, the Moon is moving slowly farther from the Earth, and so the length of the month is also increasingly slowly.

In thousands of millions of years' time, the "day" and "month" will both increase to about 55 of our present days, and the Earth will then always keep the same face turned to the Moon, just as the Moon keeps the same face to the Earth now.

△ Astronauts put reflectors on the Moon, so that scientists can measure its distance by reflecting laser beams sent from Earth. They find that the Moon is moving away at 4 cm (1½ in) per year.

Eclipses

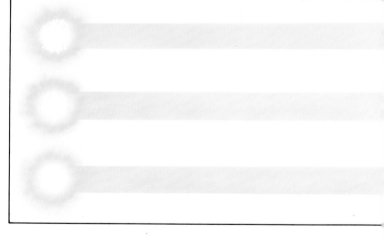

Once every year or two, you'll notice something odd about a Full Moon. One edge of the brilliant disc becomes darkened; and then this darkness creeps over the Moon, until – after an hour or so – the Moon fades from sight. All that you can see is a faint, dull reddish disc.

A little later, the opposite edge of the Moon begins to light up; and after another hour the Moon is back to its former glory.

This is an eclipse of the Moon. It happens when the Moon moves into the Earth's shadow, and our planet blocks off the sunlight that normally lights up the Moon. The Earth's shadow is the band of darkness that seems to creep across the Moon, although it is actually the Moon that is moving.

When the Moon is completely within the Earth's shadow, all the Sun's light should be cut off, and we would expect the Moon to go completely black. But our atmosphere bends some sunlight around the edge of the Earth, so that a little light does fall on the Moon even in mid-eclipse. As this light travels past the Earth, the atmosphere allows only the red rays to get through, so the eclipsed Moon appears red.

An astronaut standing on the Moon during an eclipse would see the Earth blotting out the Sun, with the edge of the Earth ringed by the red light being bent by the atmosphere.

We do not see an eclipse at every Full Moon, because the orbit of the Moon is tilted, and the

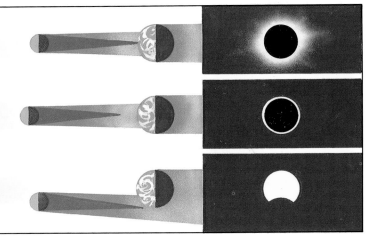

◁ The Moon hides the Sun entirely during a total eclipse (top); but it covers only the central part in an annular eclipse (center) and part of the edge in a partial eclipse (bottom).

△ The Moon is eclipsed by the Earth's shadow. You can see an eclipse of the Moon from anywhere on the night-side of the Earth, so it is more often seen than an eclipse of the Sun.

Eclipses of the Moon		
Date	**Type**	**Visible from**
Oct 17, 1986	Total	Europe, Asia, Africa, Australia
Aug 27, 1988	Partial	W of America (North, Central and South), Pacific, Australia
Feb 20, 1989	Total	NW of North America, Asia, Australia, NE Europe
Aug 17, 1989	Total	Europe, Asia, Africa, Australia
Feb 9, 1990	Total	Europe, Asia, Africa, Australia
Aug 6, 1990	Partial	Australia, Pacific, S and E Asia
Dec 21, 1991	Partial	North and Central America, Pacific, Asia, Australia
June 15, 1992	Partial	North, Central and South America
Dec 9–10, 1992	Total	Europe, Asia; North, Central and South America

Moon usually passes either above or below the Earth's shadow.

When the Moon comes between the Sun and the Earth, the Moon's shadow is thrown on to the Earth. Because the Moon is smaller than our planet, this shadow does not cover the entire Earth, and only people within the area of the shadow see an eclipse. If you are in the center of the shadow, you see the most spectacular of all sky-sights: a total eclipse of the Sun. All the Sun's light is blocked out by the Moon, and day is turned into night.

Mapping the Moon

△ Galileo's small telescopes gave him a view no better than we see with a modern pair of binoculars. But Galileo was the first astronomer to interpret his observations scientifically.
▽ Galileo's 1610 drawing of the Moon shows mountains and a large crater.

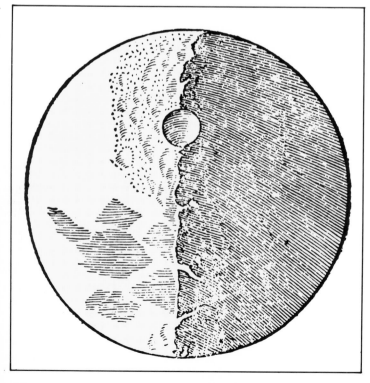

Even without a telescope, you can see some details on the Moon: the large dark patches making up the face of the "Man in the Moon."

One of the first astronomers to look through a telescope at the Moon was Sir William Lower, who described the rough surface as looking like a pie that his cook had baked! Galileo made the first accurate drawings of the Moon in 1610. He found that the dark areas were flat plains, and he rather confusingly called them seas – or *maria* (singular *mare*) in Latin.

With better telescopes, later astronomers could see more details. In 1647 a Polish astronomer, Johannes Hevelius, drew a map showing 250 plains and craters – the bowl-shaped features on the Moon.

The names we use today date from a map published by the Italian astronomer Giovanni Riccioli in 1651. He gave the flat plains poetic names like the Sea of Nectar and the Bay of Rainbows. He also named the bigger craters after famous astronomers, philosophers and scientists. Two prominent craters near the center of the Moon's disc, for example, were called Copernicus and Kepler, after the two astronomers who showed that the Earth goes around the Sun. Riccioli gave many of the craters the tongue-twisting names of ancient Greek philosophers, like Eratosthenes.

Later astronomers measured the positions of the Moon's mountains, valleys and craters so accurately that in the eighteenth century scientists had maps of the Moon that were more detailed than the maps of remote parts of the Earth like central Africa. In 1878 one astronomer published a lunar map showing 32,856 different craters, mountains and valleys.

In the twentieth century, astronomers were able to photograph the Moon, and could measure the positions of its features even more accurately. But even the best maps made from the Earth only show the half of the Moon that faces us, plus a few more features just over the edge: the far side was unknown until space probes photographed it.

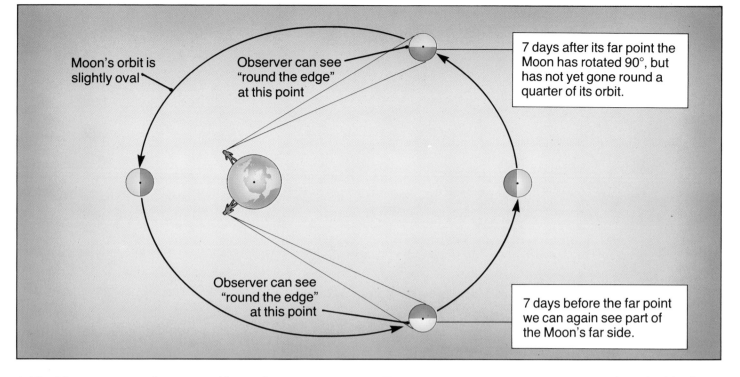

Moon's orbit is slightly oval

Observer can see "round the edge" at this point

7 days after its far point the Moon has rotated 90°, but has not yet gone round a quarter of its orbit.

Observer can see "round the edge" at this point

7 days before the far point we can again see part of the Moon's far side.

△ The Moon rotates on its axis at a constant rate, but its speed around its orbit changes. When the Moon is between its nearest and furthest points, its rotation and its motion around the orbit are out of step, and we can see part of the far side that is normally hidden. This effect is known as libration.

▽ As well as landing on the Moon, the Apollo astronauts took hundreds of photographs from orbit around the Moon, to provide better maps of the lunar surface. In this view from Apollo 14 the Earth appears as a crescent in the sky behind a heavily cratered region of the Moon's surface.

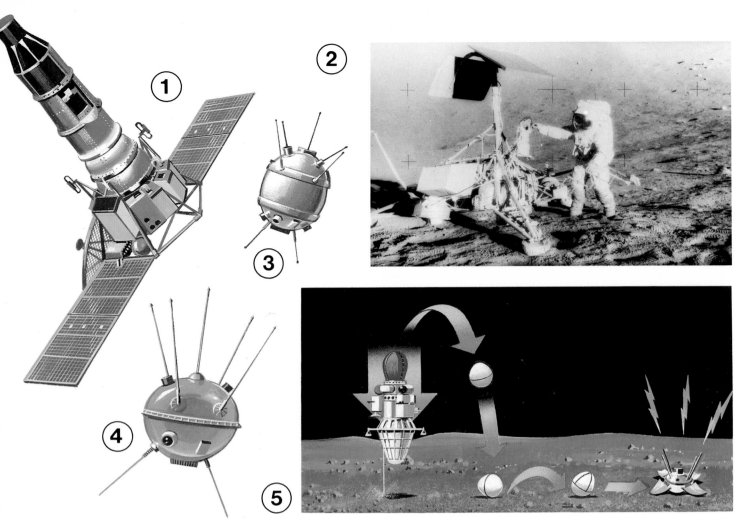

Moon probes

△ **1** Ranger 7 took the first close-up pictures of the Moon as it crash-landed.
2 Apollo 12 astronauts landed close to the unmanned Surveyor 3.
3 Luna 2, the first man-made object to reach the Moon.
4 Luna 1.
5 Luna 9 sent back the first pictures from the Moon's

People have always dreamed of flying to the Moon, and the first science-fiction stories told of adventurers meeting strange creatures there.

But the actual first steps to the Moon came in a much less dramatic way, with a series of unmanned craft.

The Russians were the first to send spaceprobes to the Moon. In 1957 they had launched the first satellite, Sputnik 1, into orbit around the Earth, and just over a year later, they sent Luna 1 across the great gulf of space toward the Moon. Luna 1 missed the Moon by 5,000 km (3,000 miles); but it gave the Russians experience in navigating across space.

The experience meant that they could head Luna 2 straight for the Moon. On September 13, 1959, Luna 2 smashed into the lunar surface, near to the crater Archimedes. It was the first man-made object to reach another world.

More important was Luna 3, which went around the back of the Moon a month later, and took the first pictures of the far side. Luna 3 surprised astronomers by showing that the Moon's far side does not have the large dark plains that we see on the near side.

The Americans sent a series of crash-landing probes, the Rangers, which took pictures as they plummeted to the Moon's surface in 1964 and 1965.

The Soviet probe Luna 9 was the first to soft-land on the Moon's surface and send back pictures. It showed a gently rolling plain, covered with small rocks. In the same year, 1966, the Americans landed the first of their soft-landing Surveyors. Later that year, the American Orbiter craft started photographing the Moon from orbit, to look for places where astronauts could land safely.

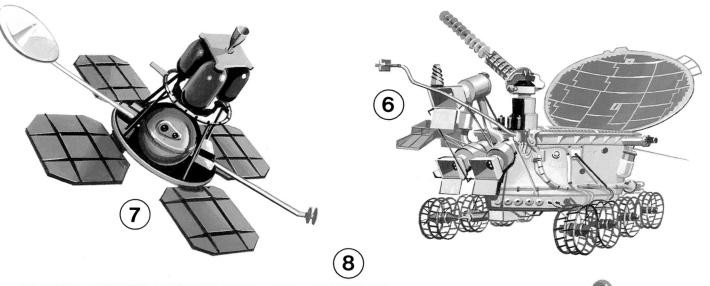

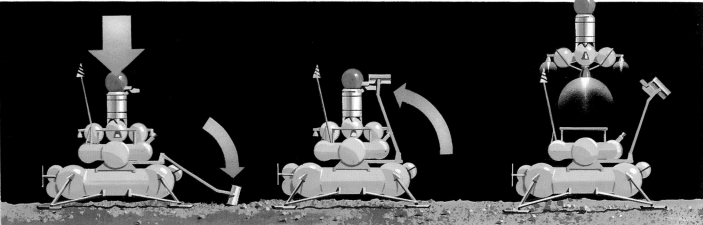

surface: the instrument capsule was ejected from the mother craft, and, after rolling over, "petals" opened to reveal the camera and antennae.

6 The eight-wheeled Lunokhod traveled over the Moon by remote control, taking pictures.
7 The American Orbiter craft.

8 The Russian Luna 16 had a drill on a long arm: it picked up a sample of soil, and put it in a container that was then blasted off back to Earth.

▽ The American and Russian probes landed in many different sites:
1 Ranger.
2 Surveyor.
3 Apollo. **4** Luna.

After the Russians were beaten in the "Moon-race" to land an astronaut on the Moon, they carried on with more sophisticated robot landers. Two of their craft carried an unmanned rover, called Lunokhod, which explored the regions around their respective landings for several months. Lunokhod 1, which landed aboard Luna 17, traveled for 11 km (7 miles), while the second Lunokhod (aboard Luna 21) went for 37 km (23 miles) over the rough lunar surface inside the crater Le Monnier.

Three of the Lunas were even able to send samples of lunar soil back to Earth completely automatically. The Luna lander had a drill, which dug out a sample of soil, and a small rocket on top, which sent the sample back to Earth. Between them, these three Lunas (numbers 16, 20 and 24) sent 300 grams (12 oz) of lunar soil back to Earth for analysis.

● **1**
■ **2**
▲ **3**
★ **4**

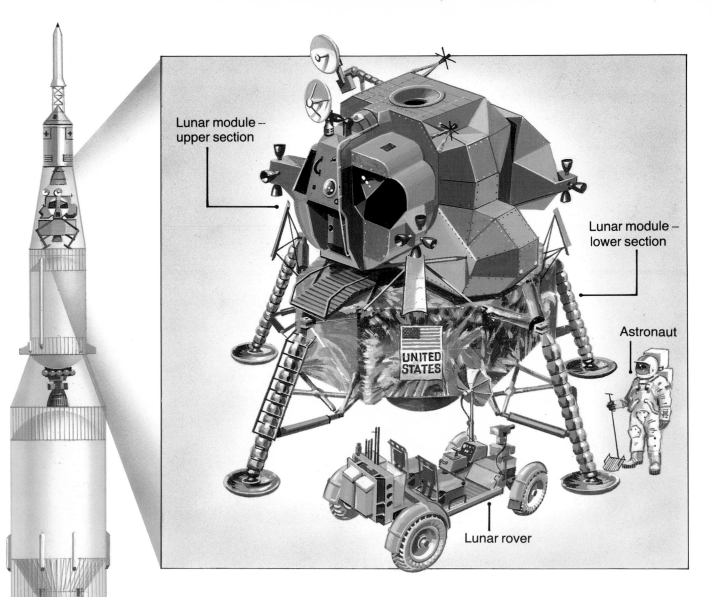

Lunar module – upper section

Lunar module – lower section

Astronaut

UNITED STATES

Lunar rover

Man on the Moon

◁ The enormous Saturn 5 rocket, built to send astronauts to the Moon, was 111 m (363 ft) high. The astronauts landed in the Lunar Module (above), which was as high as a 2-story house.

"That's one small step for a man, one giant leap for mankind." With these words, Neil Armstrong became the first person to set foot on another world. The date was July 20, 1969, and Armstrong's "small step" marked the culmination of eight years' frantic effort by the United States to beat the Russians to the Moon.

The first Russian spaceman, Yuri Gagarin, was launched in 1961. This persuaded President John F. Kennedy that the United States should try to get to the Moon first. In 1962, the first American, John Glenn, went into orbit, in a capsule called Mercury.

After three more Mercury flights, the Americans began launching the larger Gemini capsules, which each contained two astronauts.

△ Astronaut Jack Schmitt scoops up some lunar soil. The spacesuit weighs as much as the astronaut, but is easy to cope with under the low gravity.

▷ A makeshift repair to the fender of the Lunar Rover carried by Apollo 17. The rover carried the astronauts 35 km (22 miles) at 14 km/h (9 mph).

The Moon flights were called Apollo, and each involved three astronauts. They lived in a conical capsule, the Command Module, which was attached to a large cylinder, the Service Module, that supplied them with oxygen, water and electrical power. There was also a Lunar Module, a spidery-looking device that actually went down to land on the Moon.

In December 1968, an Apollo crew flew around the Moon. They read Christmas messages from above the Moon's surface.

The following July, Neil Armstrong set off, with Buzz Aldrin and Mike Collins. When they were in orbit around the Moon, Collins stayed in the Command Module, while Armstrong and Aldrin climbed into the Lunar Module.

Armstrong flew the module down to the lunar surface and stepped out, to become the first man on the Moon. Armstrong and Aldrin stayed on the Moon for 2½ hours. They set up scientific instruments and collected rocks.

The top section of the Lunar Module blasted them back into space to rejoin Collins. The three journeyed back to Earth in the Command Module, splashing down in the sea.

There were five more successful Apollo missions, which landed in different parts of the Moon in the years 1969 to 1972. The one failure was Apollo 13, which suffered an explosion in its Service Module. The astronauts were lucky to get back to Earth alive.

The twelve astronauts who walked on the Moon left behind a range of scientific instruments, to measure the Moon's magnetism, to record moonquakes, and to measure any gases that the Moon might emit. They also brought back rocks for geologists to analyze.

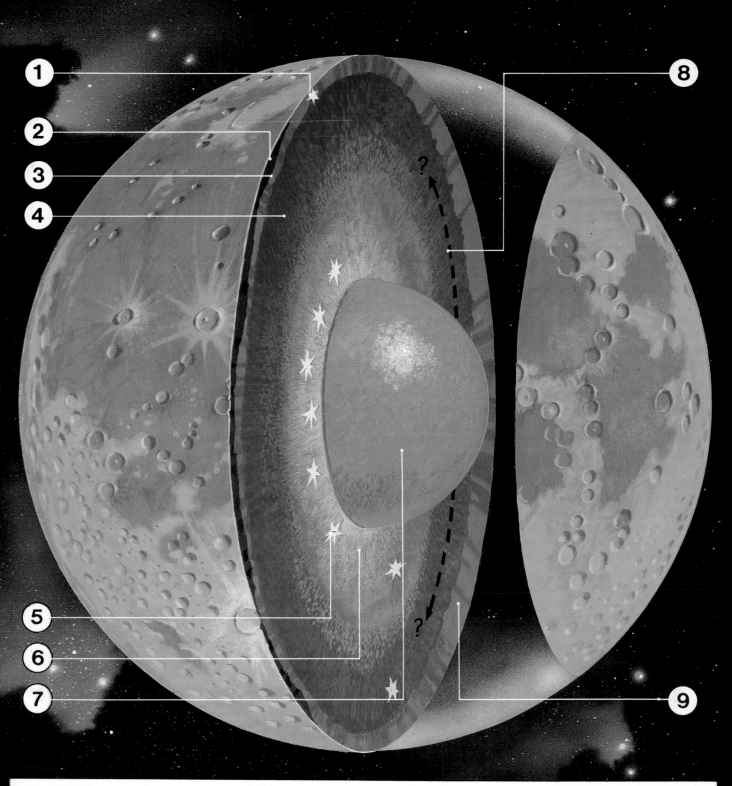

1

2

3

4

8

5

6

7

9

?

?

△ The Apollo seismometers found "shallow moonquakes" (**1**) which occur less than 300 km (200 miles) below the surface. In the distant past, rocks below the surface melted and oozed out on to the surface as basalts (**2**), as much as 5 km (3 miles) deep, that make up the dark lava plains. The Moon's solid crust (**3**) is made of light-colored anorthosites (a rock rather like granite on the Earth), the type of rock exposed in the lunar highlands: it is 60 km (37 miles) thick. Below the crust is the mantle (**4**), consisting of solid rock that is more like basalt. Eight hundred km (500 miles) down is a region that produces the "deep moonquakes" (**5**) measured by the Apollo instruments. This coincides with a partly molten zone (**6**) at the bottom of the mantle. At the Moon's very center, there may be a core (**7**) made of iron, but geologists still do not agree about its existence. Accurate measurements of the Moon's gravity reveal places where there is a concentration of matter just below the surface: a "mascon" (**8**). The crust on the far side of the Moon (**9**) is much thicker (145 km, 90 miles). This has prevented basalt from oozing out and forming lava plains on the far side.

Inside the Moon

The six Apollo missions have revealed a lot of new information, not only about the surface of the Moon, but also about its interior.

The astronauts brought back a total of over a third of a tonne of assorted Moon rocks. Geologists have been able to sort these into different kinds and measure their ages. They have found that the oldest parts of the Moon are the bright highland regions, where the rocks have not altered for over 4,000 million years.

The dark plains (or *maria*) are regions where molten rock, or lava, has flowed out and filled the lower-lying areas. The last flows of lava stopped about 3,000 million years ago.

The rocks also show that the Moon's craters were not formed by volcanoes, as some astronomers had believed. The craters were blasted out by large meteorites hitting the Moon. Most of the Moon's large craters were created over 3,500 million years ago, but some are more recent.

△ Under the microscope, a section of lunar rock shows many different kinds of crystals, made of different chemical compounds. By studying the elements in these crystals, geologists can work out the age of the rock, when it last melted, and when it was last shattered by the impact of a meteorite.

There are many different kinds of rock lying on the Moon's surface, as astronauts found at each Apollo landing site. Many of these rocks have been thrown out from the impact of meteorites many thousands of miles away, and they provide geologists with samples of rock from regions that the astronauts (and unmanned Russian landers) never visited.

Most of the rocks are either of the old, bright highland type, or of the dark basalt from the *mare*. The Moon's geology is much simpler than the geology of the Earth, which has many other types of rock, produced either by volcanoes or by the build-up of sediments on the sea bed.

The Apollo astronauts left seismometers on the Moon's surface, to measure the strength of "moonquakes". Many geologists did not expect to find any moonquakes, because they thought the Moon had been dead for thousands of millions of years. But the instruments found moonquakes coming from deep inside the Moon and from just below the surface.

Geologists have been able to work out the internal structure of the Moon by analyzing the waves from moonquakes. These show several distinct layers of rock within the Moon, and suggest that it has a central core of iron.

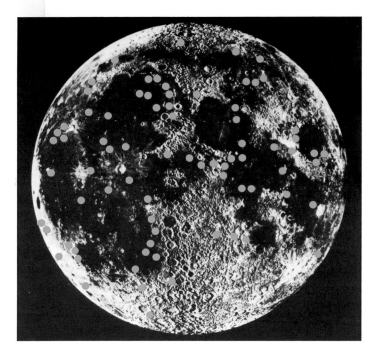

△ Astronomers sometimes see bright glows and small patches of "fog" on the supposedly lifeless and airless Moon. These Transient Lunar Phenomena (TLPs) seem to occur mainly along the edges of the *mare* plains. They may be due to gas escaping from underground pockets.

Birth of the Moon

Astronomers have always been puzzled about the way in which the Moon was born. And even the findings from the Apollo missions have not brought a conclusive answer.

The Solar System was born about 4,600 million years ago, as a swirling disc of gas and dust called a nebula. The big central "hub" became the Sun, while the outer regions of the disc condensed into the nine planets.

The oldest rock that the Apollo astronauts brought back was 4,600 million years old, so the Moon undoubtedly came into being at the same time as the Earth. According to one theory, the Moon was once part of the Earth, and split off because the Earth was rotating so rapidly. But the Apollo rock samples are rather different from the rock of the Earth's surface, so most astronomers have abandoned this idea.

The moons orbiting the other planets probably formed from swirling nebulae going around each planet, like miniature Solar Systems. But in this case the Earth should have a family of moons, like those of Jupiter, not just one Moon. In addition its orbit should not be tilted up, and the theory doesn't explain why the Moon's composition is different from the Earth's.

Other astronomers have suggested that the Moon formed as a planet in its own right, and that the Earth "captured" it when the Moon approached too closely. But it is difficult to explain how this capture occurred.

The latest theory explains the fact that the Moon's rocks are slightly different from the Earth's by the idea that a giant meteorite hit the Earth, and splashed out matter that later condensed into the Moon. In the process, some elements evaporated into space, so changing the composition of the Moon's rocks.

Three theories of the Moon's birth

1 Nebula
When the Solar System formed from a giant swirling disc of gas and dust, individual whirls turned into the planets. The gases around each planet condensed into moons. Some planets acquired a system of moons, but the material around the Earth formed into a single Moon.

2 Capture
The Moon formed as a separate planet, rather closer to the Sun than the Earth. The Moon's orbit crossed the path of the Earth – just as the orbit of Pluto crosses that of Neptune. When the Moon came too close, the Earth's gravity swung it around into an orbit around the Earth.

3 Moonsplash
A giant meteorite hit the Earth in its early days and splashed rock into space. Many of these rock fragments went into orbit as miniature moons, forming a ring around the Earth – rather like the rings of Saturn. These rocks gradually came together and built up into the Moon.

Other moons

△ Our Moon (**1**) is very "dead" and uninteresting when compared to the other planets' moons. Jupiter's moon Io (**2**) has active volcanoes. Phobos and Deimos (**3**), Mars's moons, are small and potato-shaped. Among Jupiter's other moons, Europa (**4**) has a smooth, white, icy surface;

The Earth is far from being the only planet with a moon. In fact, all the planets except for Mercury and Venus have moons going around them. The Earth is also a poor relation in having only one moon: Uranus has 15 moons, Jupiter 16, and Saturn more than 20!

The Earth is quite unusual in having a moon that is so large in comparison to the planet's own size, and many astronomers call the Earth-Moon a double planet. Pluto is the only other double planet: its moon Charon is one-third the size of Pluto itself. But the Pluto-Charon double planet is very much a smaller sister of the Earth-Moon system – the planet Pluto itself is no larger than our Moon.

In the case of all the other planets, the planet itself is at least twenty times larger than its biggest moon, and we can clearly say that one is "the planet" and the others "the moons."

Jupiter, Saturn and Uranus have such large satellite families that they are like Solar Systems in miniature. And even if these moons are small compared to the giant planet in charge, they are still large worlds in their own right. Four of them are bigger than the Earth's Moon.

The largest moon in the Solar System is Ganymede, which orbits Jupiter. With a diameter of 5,262 km (3,270 miles) Ganymede is 50% larger than our Moon. Only slightly smaller is Saturn's biggest moon, Titan. Both these worlds are actually bigger than two of the planets, Mercury and Pluto. Titan is the only moon with a substantial atmosphere.

Two more of Jupiter's moons – Callisto and volcanic Io – are also larger than our Moon. Just smaller than our Moon are Jupiter's fourth-largest moon, ice-covered Europa, and Neptune's Triton.

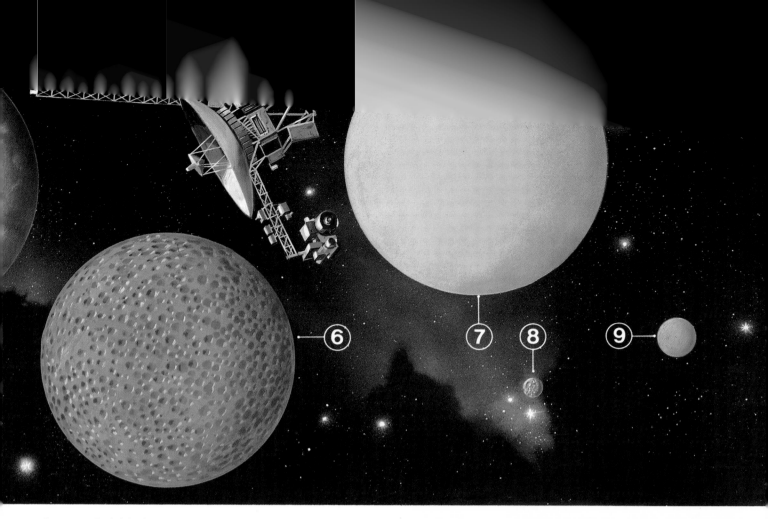

Ganymede (**5**) is the largest moon of all, and Callisto (**6**) is even more cratered than our Moon. Saturn's largest moon, Titan (**7**) has orange clouds that hide its surface from view; Mimas (**8**), has a huge crater on its surface. Astronomers did not discover Pluto's moon Charon (**9**) until 1978.

Neptune is so far away that we know very little about Triton, but some astronomers suspect it may have seas of liquefied gases. The Voyager 2 spaceprobe will find out when it passes Neptune and Triton in August 1989.

Most of the other moons are much smaller, some of them just a few miles across. Many of them are not spherical in shape: Saturn's moon Hyperion looks like a giant hamburger. The two tiny moons of Mars may be small asteroids captured from the asteroid belt between Mars and Jupiter. Uranus has seven small moons that seem to be fragments of one moon, split up by the impact of a big meteorite.

Mars's two moons are made of rock, like our Moon. But other moons, farther away from the Sun's heat, are made of a mixture of rock and ice. Saturn's moon Enceladus is a giant "snowball," made entirely of ice.

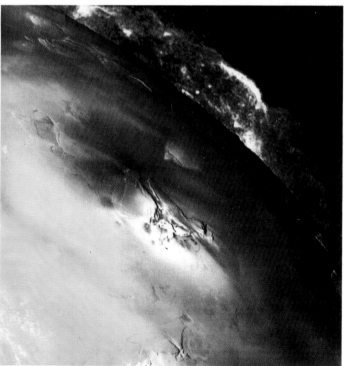

△ Jupiter's moon Io looks entirely different from our Moon. Io is covered with orange deposits of sulfur, dotted with dark lakes of molten sulfur. It has active volcanoes that shoot gases 300 km (200 miles) out into space. The energy for these volcanoes comes from the powerful pull of Jupiter's gravity.

Moonbase of the future

Clavius Base: July 20, 2019. On the fiftieth anniversary of man's first "small step" on the Moon, the first permanent colonists of the Moon have landed to take up residence in their new underground base, set in the huge crater Clavius, near the Moon's south pole.

Planning for this base started thirty years ago. The last of the Apollo astronauts had left the Moon in December 1972, and by the late 1980s astronomers and other scientists were arguing that it was time to return to the Moon.

The Americans saw this as the next step beyond their Space Station, which was completed in 1995. They were backed by the Europeans and Japanese, who wanted to build on their brilliantly successful – but unmanned – spaceprobes to Halley's Comet in 1986 by sending astronauts to the Moon. After the Russians had pulled off a propaganda coup by

sending cosmonauts around Mars in 1999, they joined in the project too – realizing that a manned Mars base was too ambitious.

The planners got a big stimulus in 1994, when a Japanese probe, sent over the Moon's poles, discovered the first traces of water on the Moon – frozen into patches of ice on crater-walls that were never exposed to the Sun. The large ice deposits in Clavius made it an ideal choice for the first lunar base.

From the start, the planners had seen the moonbase as a commercial proposition, as well as a scientific base. The Apollo missions had shown that the Moon's rocks are rich in useful metals, such as aluminum, chromium, magnesium and manganese. With the Moon's low gravity, and lack of atmosphere, it is easy to launch materials into space, where they can be used to build new space stations and spacecraft.

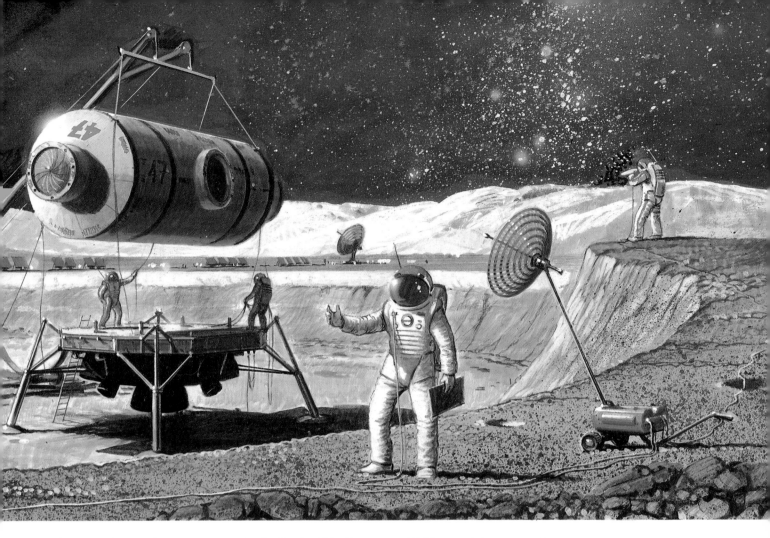

△ Construction workers unload a module of the lunar base, from the descent stage that landed it on the Moon. This module was made at a space station in Earth-orbit. Once the lunar mines and factories are operating, future parts of the moonbase will be made on the Moon.

▽ The module is buried under 2 m (6 ft) of loose soil to protect the colonists from the hot and cold of the lunar day and night and from bursts of radiation from the Sun. Inside the module the colonists can live and work just as they do on Earth. The only noticeable difference is the low gravity.

Factories now being built on the Moon can also extract oxygen from the rocks and send this gas to the space stations. This provides a supply of air more easily than bringing it up from the Earth.

As well as engineers and miners, the first colonists naturally include many scientists. Geologists will be studying the Moon in great detail to learn how both the Moon and the Solar System came into being. Astronomers are beginning to erect giant telescopes, taking advantage of both the Moon's clear dark skies and its low gravity.

On the far side of the Moon, where there is no radio interference from the Earth, they are turning a crater into a gigantic radio telescope. With this sensitive radio "ear," they hope to pick up the first signals from alien civilizations on planets circling other stars.

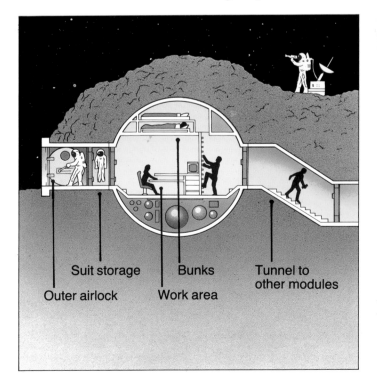

Suit storage

Outer airlock

Bunks

Work area

Tunnel to other modules

Moon map

0 250 500 km

0 155 310 miles

This map shows the side of the Moon that always faces the Earth. With the naked eye you can make out the big dark plains (the "seas"); binoculars will reveal the largest craters. A telescope will show you all the craters named on this map. (It will also make the Moon appear upside-down.)

Craters

1 Albategnius
2 Alphonsus
3 Archimedes
4 Aristarchus
5 Aristoteles
6 Arzachel
7 Atlas
8 Cassini
9 Catharina
10 Clavius
11 Copernicus
12 Eratosthenes
13 Fracastorius
14 Fra Mauro
15 Grimaldi
16 Hipparchus
17 Kepler
18 Langrenus
19 Longomontanus
20 Maginus
21 Maurolycus
22 Piccolomini
23 Plato
24 Ptolomaeus
25 Pitatus
26 Theophilus
27 Tycho

Seas, bays and oceans

28 Mare Crisium
   Sea of Crises
29 Mare Fecunditatis
   Sea of Fertility
30 Mare Frigoris
   Sea of Cold
31 Mare Humorum
   Sea of Humors
32 Mare Imbrium
   Sea of Rains
33 Mare Nectaris
   Sea of Nectar
34 Mare Nubium
   Sea of Clouds
35 Mare Serenitatis
   Sea of Serenity
36 Mare Tranquillitatis
   Sea of Tranquillity
37 Mare Vaporum
   Sea of Vapors
38 Oceanus Procelarum
   Ocean of Storms
39 Sinus Iridum
   Bay of Rainbows
40 Sinus Roris
   Bay of Dews

Mountain ranges

41 Apennines
42 Caucasus
43 Haemus
44 Jura
45 Taurus

The Moon's far side

This is the side of the Moon that we can never see from the Earth. Russia's Luna 3 first photographed the far side in 1959. Since then, it has been photographed by other unmanned spaceprobes, and also by the Apollo astronauts as they flew around the Moon. The far side does not have any of the big dark lava plains ("seas") that we see on the side that faces the Earth: it is a continuous jumble of craters of all sizes. These craters have been named after scientists and rocket pioneers.

Looking at the Moon

There's always plenty to see on the Moon, and it is always changing as sunlight catches the surface at different angles. The worst time to observe is at Full Moon: although all the Moon is lit up, there's little contrast. At other times, the shadows show up details in the craters.

Use a soft pencil to sketch the "seas", mountains and craters that you can see through binoculars or telescope. You'll see them best near the terminator, the edge of the sunlit region.

These two amateur photos were taken using equipment like that shown opposite. If you take several pictures a couple of minutes apart, without moving the camera, the rotation of the Earth will produce a row of Moons!

Photographing the Moon
An ordinary camera lens gives a disappointing view of the Moon, as a very small spot on the film. To get a reasonable picture, you need a telephoto lens with a focal length of at least 300 mm. Support the camera and lens on a tripod; set the focus to infinity, the f-stop to its smallest number, and the camera to automatic.

Even the smallest telescope will give you superb views of the Moon; in a big 'scope, it will feel as though you are flying over the Moon's surface. Make sure the telescope has a firm mount, or the picture will wobble.

Occultations

The Moon sometimes moves in front of a distant planet or star, and hides (occults) it. When the Moon occults a planet like Saturn (**1**), you can see just how much smaller and fainter the planet appears, because of its distance. If a star is right at the edge of the Moon (**2**), you can see it disappear and reappear behind the Moon's mountains (**3**). When the dark side of the Moon is heading toward a star (**4**), you cannot see where the edge of the Moon is, and the star will disappear quite unexpectedly.

Suitable films

You will need a fairly fast film, with an ASA/ISO number of 100 or more. A higher ASA/ISO number (say 400) will allow a shorter exposure, but it will not show quite as much detail.

100 ASA film is a good all-round type.

400 ASA film gives a slightly "grainy" look to your pictures.

Glossary

Anorthosite A type of rock that makes up the lunar highlands: similar to granite.

Apollo The series of American manned flights to the Moon: the crew of Apollo 11 were the first to land. The last was Apollo 17 in 1972.

Atmosphere The layer of gases surrounding a planet or moon: Earth's Moon has no atmosphere.

Basalt A dark rock that consists of solidified lava.

Centrifugal force A force that acts outwards from the center of a spinning body.

Crater A bowl-shaped depression that is caused by the impact of a meteorite on the Moon (or other body).

Crescent The appearance of the Moon as a thin sliver.

Double planet A pair of similarly sized bodies orbiting the Sun together: examples are the Earth and Moon, and Pluto and Charon.

Eclipse The effect caused when one celestial body casts a shadow on another. In an eclipse of the Moon, the Moon moves into the Earth's shadow. An eclipse of the Sun occurs when the Moon's shadow falls on the Earth.

Far side The part of the Moon that is never seen from the Earth.

First quarter The appearance of the Moon half lit-up, before Full Moon.

Full Moon The appearance of the Moon totally lit up.

Gibbous The appearance of the Moon more than half lit-up.

Gravity The force that pulls objects together, toward the center of the Moon or a planet. Its strength depends on the amount of matter in the body, and on its size: the Moon's gravity is only one-sixth that of the Earth.

Highlands The lighter-colored, heavily cratered parts of the Moon.

Laser A device that produces an intense beam of light.

Last quarter The appearance of the Moon as half lit-up, after Full Moon.

Libration An effect that allows us to see some of the Moon's far side, that is normally hidden.

Luna A series of Soviet unmanned probes to the Moon.

Lunar Related to the Moon.

Lunokhod A Soviet unmanned lunar rover.

Man in the Moon The appearance of a face in the Full Moon, caused by the disposition of the dark plains.

Mare (plural maria). A dark plain on the Moon, consisting of solidified lava.

Mascon A concentration of matter just below the Moon's surface, which is revealed by its extra gravitational pull.

Meteorite A chunk of rock orbiting the Sun that strikes a moon or planet.

Module A section of a space station or moonbase.

Month The time from one Full Moon to the next ($29\frac{1}{2}$ days).

Moonquake The equivalent of an earthquake on the Moon.

Nebula A cloud of gas and dust in space.

New Moon The time when the Moon is on the sunward side of the Earth and is not visible.

Occultation The hiding of one celestial body behind another.

Orbit The path of one object around another.

◁ Craters of all sizes litter the Moon's surface. The "hills" here are actually the walls of the large adjoining craters Fra Mauro and Parry, some 80 km (50 miles) across. The Apollo 14 astronauts who took this picture landed here in 1971.

Finding out more

△ The Apollo 17 Command Module (conical section on the right) attached to the cylindrical Service Module, photographed by astronauts in the Lunar Module. The open section contains cameras and other instruments to scrutinize the Moon's surface.

Orbiter A series of American unmanned spacecraft that photographed the Moon from orbit around it.

Phases The differing shapes of the Moon (or other celestial body) as we see different amounts lit up by the Sun.

Plains The flat regions of the Moon, consisting of solidified lava.

Radio telescope A sensitive radio receiver for picking up weak signals from space.

Ranger A series of American probes that photographed the Moon as they crash-landed.

Satellite A small object orbiting a larger one: the Moon is the Earth's satellite.

Saturn 5 The rocket used for the Apollo Moon flights.

Solar System The system of planets and other bodies orbiting the Sun.

Surveyor A series of American unmanned probes that soft-landed on the Moon.

Terminator The line between the sunlit and dark parts of the Moon (or other body).

Tides The twice-daily rise and fall of the seas, caused by the influence of the Moon.

Transient Lunar Phenomenon A small, temporary patch of fog or colored gas on the Moon.

Vacuum A complete lack of gas or any other substance.

Voyager A pair of unmanned American spaceprobes that photographed Jupiter, Saturn and Uranus and their moons.

Waning The shrinking appearance of the Moon, after Full Moon.

Waxing The growing appearance of the Moon, between New Moon and Full Moon.

The observatories run by professional astronomers do not spend much time studying the Moon: their telescopes are looking at distant planets, stars and galaxies. You can find out more about the Moon at a planetarium, a museum or even at your local astronomical society run by amateur astronomers.

In the US the leading society for people who are really serious about observing the Moon is the Association of Lunar and Planetary Observers (ALPO) at 8930 Raven Drive, Waco, Texas 76710. In Canada the main astronomical society is the Royal Astronomical Society of Canada, 124 Merton Street, Toronto, Ontario, Canada M45 2Z2. Both of these, however, are for people with quite a bit of knowledge, and you may feel happier joining a local club or society first. You can find out whether there's one near you by writing to the Astronomical League, c/o Carole J. Beaman, Editor, *The Reflector*, 6804 Alvina Road, Rockford, Ill. 61103. *The Reflector* carries news of local society events. Many of these societies have a moderate sized telescope that you can use to observe the Moon for yourself.

Either one of the national societies or a local society will be very happy to give you practical advice on sketching craters, photographing the Moon, timing when occultations take place, and looking out for the rare Transient Lunar Phenomena.

One of the best places to visit for learning more about the Moon, and especially about its motion and its phases, is a planetarium. There isn't space to give a detailed list here, but you'll find some of the biggest in the following cities: Chicago, Los Angeles, New York, Salt Lake City, Toronto, Tucson, Vancouver.

The Air and Space Museum in Washington, D.C., has the world's most comprehensive display of the unmanned and manned craft that went to the Moon, and a sample of Moon rock that you can actually touch. You can also see displays of the Mercury, Gemini and Apollo programs – including a full-size Saturn 5 rocket – at the Kennedy Space Center, Cape Canaveral, Florida.

Index

32

PRINTED IN BELGIUM BY

proost
INTERNATIONAL BOOK PRODUCTION